Early to Mid-Elementary

Christmas Carols for Kids

10 Piano Solos with Optional Accompaniments

Arranged by Carolyn C. Setliff

ISBN 978-1-4950-9728-7

WILLIS MUSIC

EXCLUSIVELY DISTRIBUTED BY

HAL•LEONARD®

Visit Hal Leonard Online at
www.halleonard.com

Preface

Christmas always brings back happy memories of family times together celebrating the joy of the season with special dinners, family reunions, and of course, music.

In this special holiday season, I hope you will plan time to share your gift of music with your family, friends, and those who would appreciate some special Christmas cheer.

These favorites of mine are arranged to be played as solos by the student or as duets with a parent or older sibling. May your Christmas be filled with joy!

Carolyn C. Setliff

Contents

The First Noel

17th Century English Carol
Arranged by Carolyn C. Setliff

Moderato

The _ first _ No - el, the _ an - gel did say was to

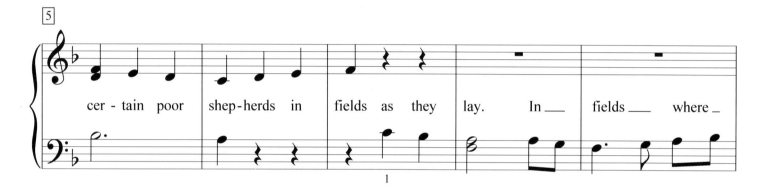

cer - tain poor shep-herds in fields as they lay. In _ fields _ where _

Accompaniment (Student plays one octave higher than written.)

Moderato

they lay ___ keep - ing their sheep, on a cold win - ter's night ___ that

was ___ so deep. No - el, ___ No - el, No - el, No -

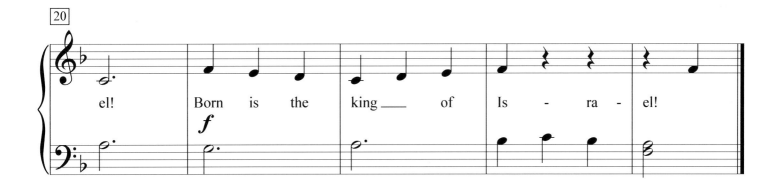

el! Born is the king ___ of Is - ra - el!

Hark! The Herald Angels Sing

Words by Charles Wesley
Altered by George Whitefield
Music by Felix Mendelssohn-Bartholdy
Arranged by William H. Cummings
Adapted by Carolyn C. Setliff

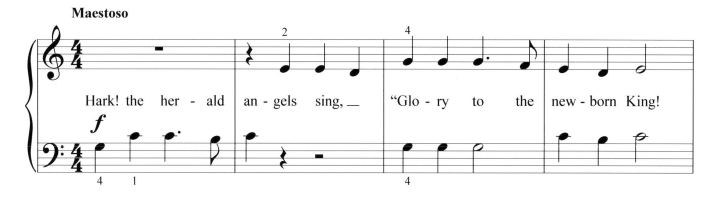

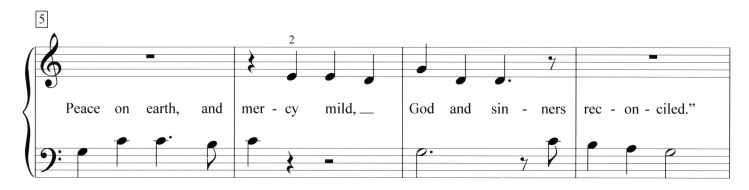

Accompaniment (Student plays one octave higher than written.)

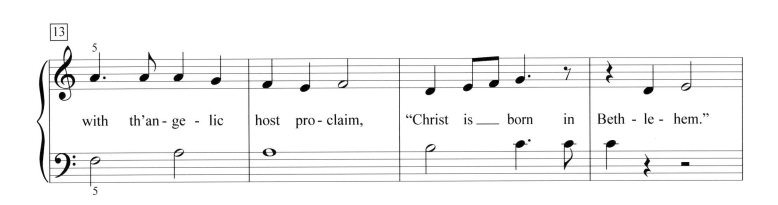

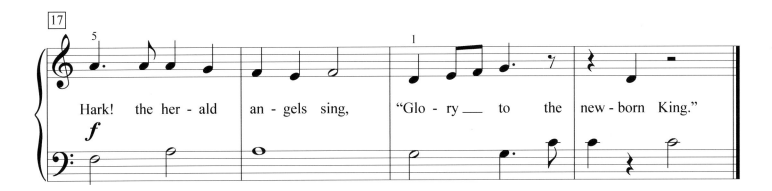

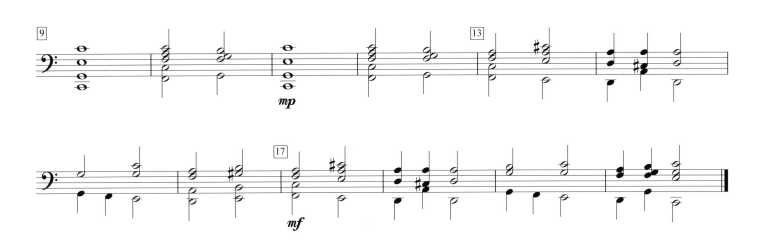

I Saw Three Ships

18th Century English Carol
Arranged by Carolyn C. Setliff

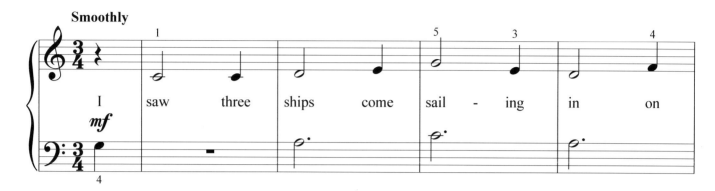

I saw three ships come sail - ing in on

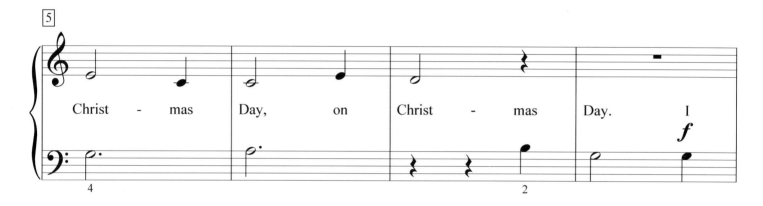

Christ - mas Day, on Christ - mas Day. I

Accompaniment (Student plays one octave higher than written.)

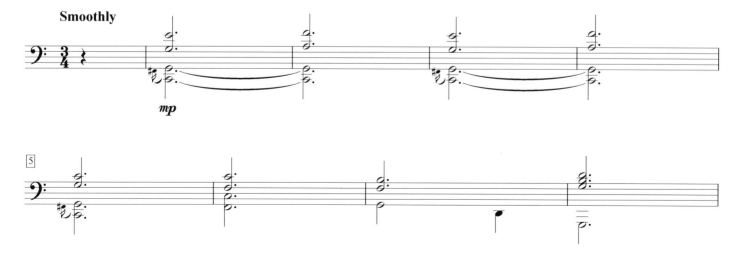

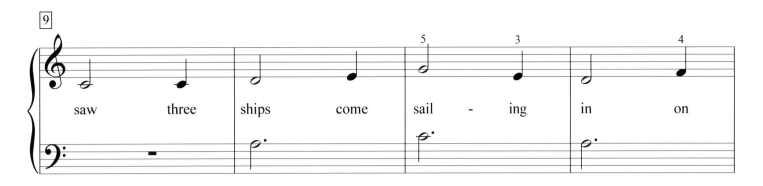

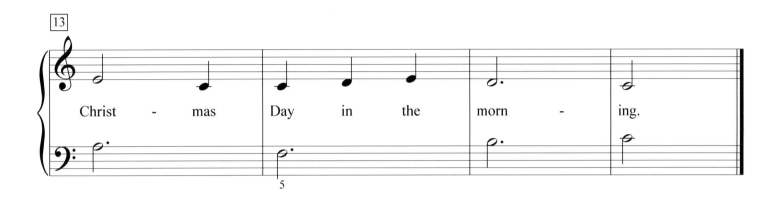

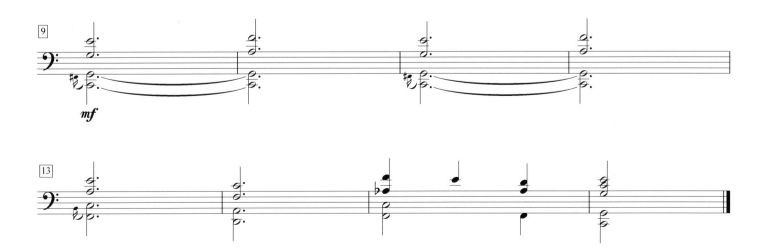

Jingle Bells

Words and Music by J. Pierpont
Arranged by Carolyn C. Setliff

Happily

Jin - gle bells, jin - gle bells, jin - gle all the way.

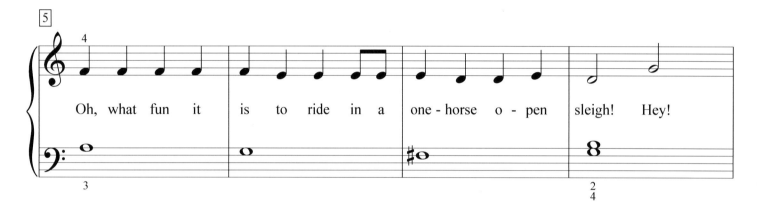

Oh, what fun it is to ride in a one - horse o - pen sleigh! Hey!

Accompaniment (Student plays one octave higher than written.)

Happily

With light pedal

Joseph Dearest, Joseph Mine

Traditional German Carol
Arranged by Carolyn C. Setliff

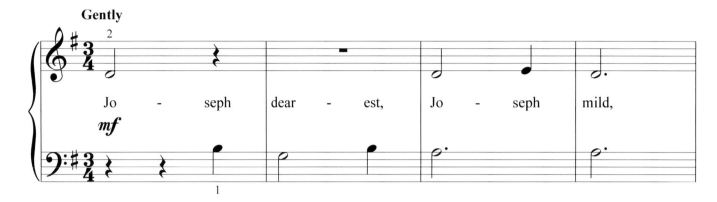

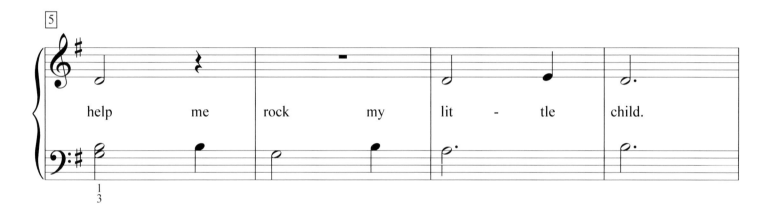

Accompaniment (Student plays one octave higher than written.)

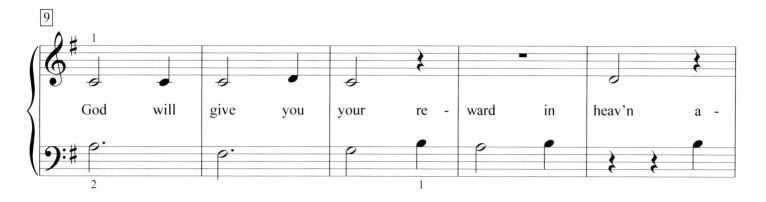

God will give you your re - ward in heav'n a -

bove. The child of Vir - gin Mar - y.

Joy to the World

Words by Isaac Watts
Music by George Frideric Handel
Adapted by Lowell Mason
Arranged by Carolyn C. Setliff

Joy to the world! The Lord is come. Let

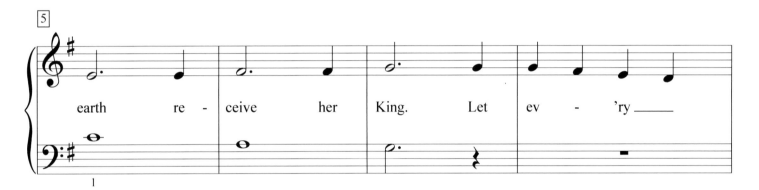

earth re - ceive her King. Let ev - 'ry _____

Accompaniment (Student plays one octave higher than written.)

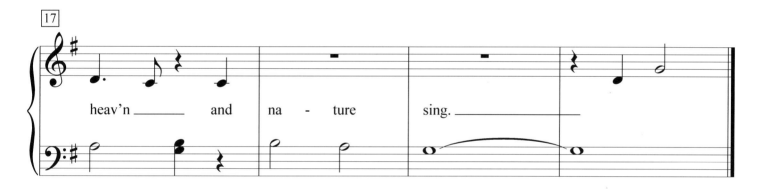

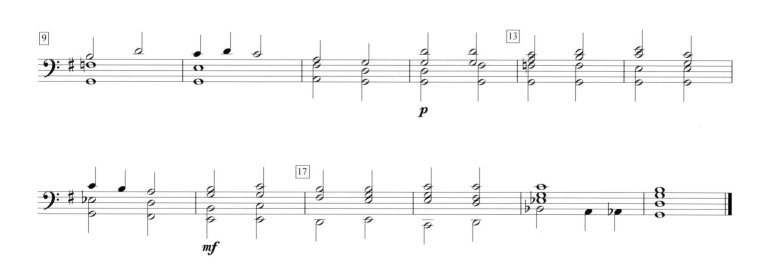

O Come, All Ye Faithful
(Adeste Fideles)

Music by John Francis Wade
Latin Words translated by Frederick Oakeley
Arranged by Carolyn C. Setliff

With adoration

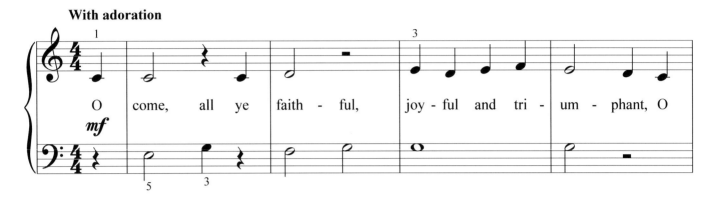

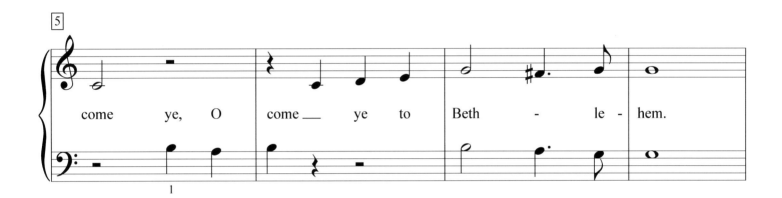

Accompaniment (Student plays one octave higher than written.)

With adoration

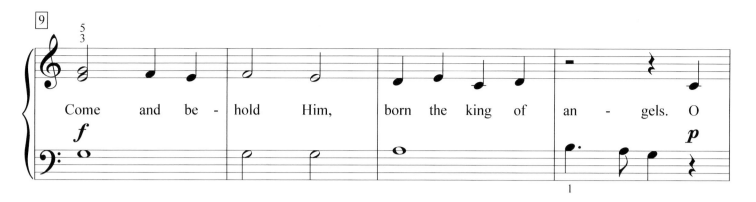

Come and be - hold Him, born the king of an - gels. O

come, let us a - dore Him, O come, let us a - dore Him, O

come, let us a - dore Him, ___ Christ ___ the Lord.

Pat-A-Pan
(Willie, Take Your Little Drum)

Words and Music by Bernard de la Monnoye
Arranged by Carolyn C. Setliff

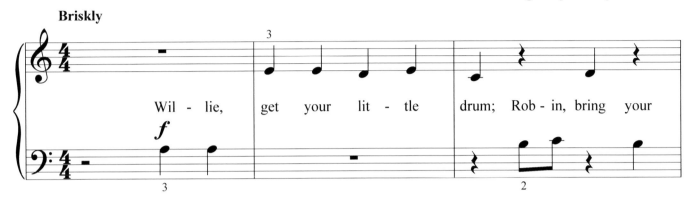

Accompaniment (Student plays one octave higher than written.)

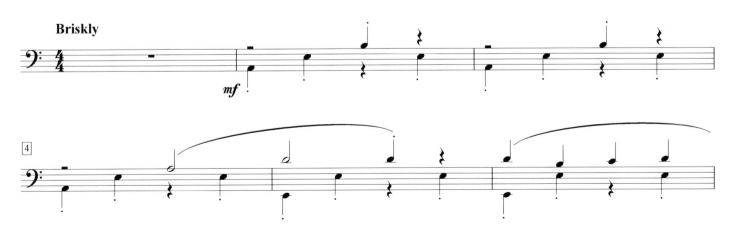

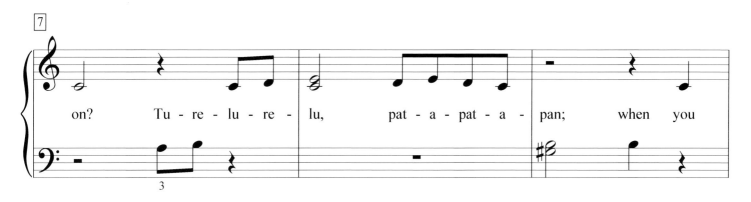

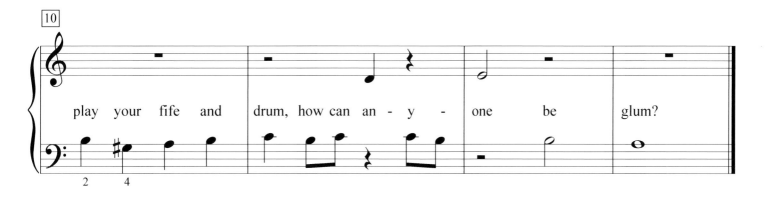

on? Tu - re - lu - re - lu, pat - a - pat - a - pan; when you

play your fife and drum, how can an - y - one be glum?

Silent Night

Words by Joseph Mohr
Translated by John F. Young
Music by Franz X. Gruber
Arranged by Carolyn C. Setliff

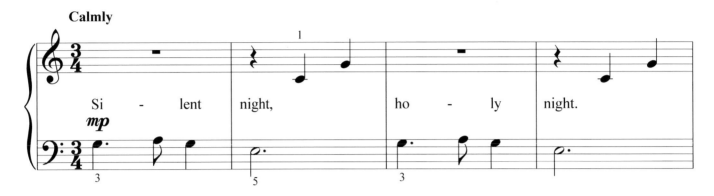

Si - lent night, ho - ly night.

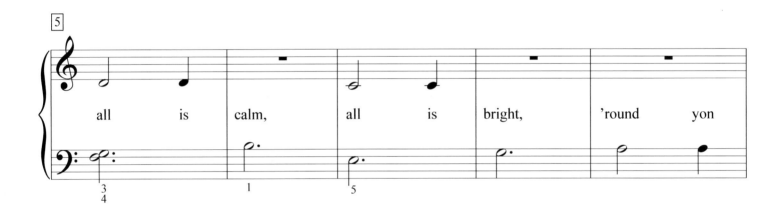

all is calm, all is bright, 'round yon

Accompaniment (Student plays one octave higher than written.)

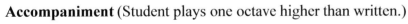

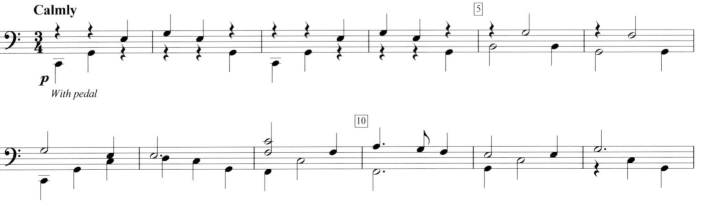

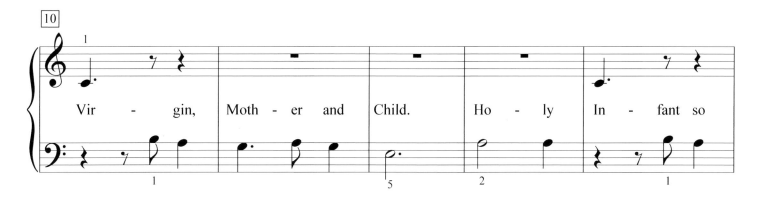

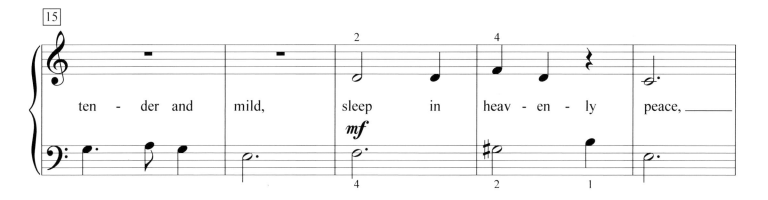

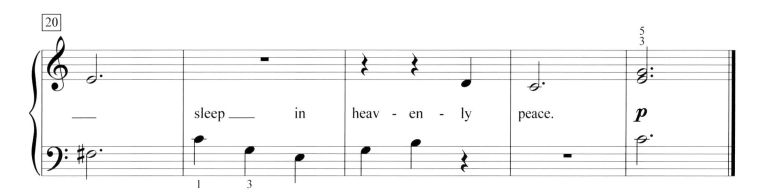

Up on the Housetop

Words and Music by B.R. Hanby
Arranged by Carolyn C. Setliff

Up on the house-top rein-deer pause, out jumps good ol'

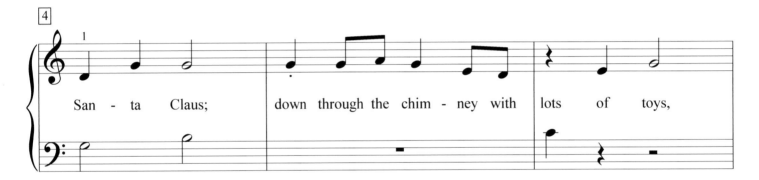

San - ta Claus; down through the chim - ney with lots of toys,

Accompaniment (Student plays one octave higher than written.)

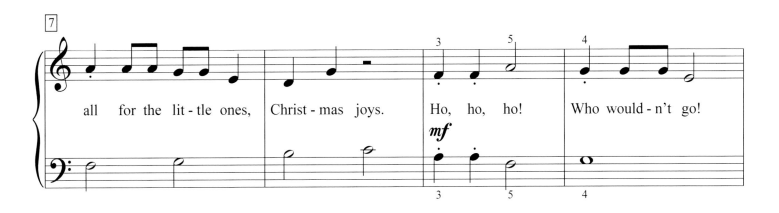

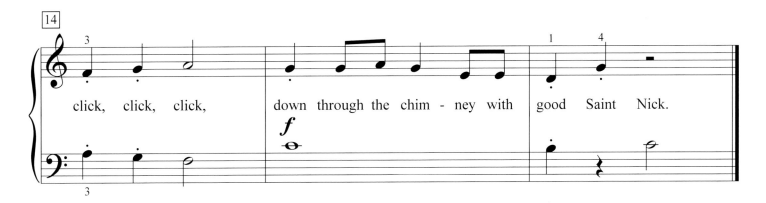

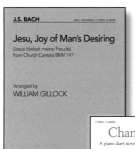

Dynamic Duets

and Exciting Ensembles from Willis Music!

SELECTED COLLECTIONS

00416804 Accent on Duets (MI-LI) /
William Gillock........................$12.99

00416822 All-American Ragtime Duets
(EI) / *Glenda Austin* $7.99

00416732 Concerto No. 1
for Piano and Strings (MI) (2P, 4H) /
Alexander Peskanov $14.95

00416898 Duets in Color Book 1 (EI-MI) /
Naoko Ikeda $12.99

00138687 5 Easy Duets (EE-ME) /
Carolyn Miller $7.99

00406230 First Piano Duets (EE) /
John Thompson series $4.95

00416805 New Orleans Jazz Styles Duets
(EI) / *Gillock, arr. Austin*............$9.99

00416830 Teaching Little Fingers Easy Duets
(EE) / *arr. Miller* $6.99

SELECTED SHEETS

Early Elementary

00125695 The Knights' Quest (1P, 4H) /
Wendy Stevens............................ $3.99

00406743 Wisteria (1P, 4H) /
Carolyn C. Setliff.........................$2.95

Mid-Elementary

00412289 Andante Theme from
"Surprise Symphony" (1P, 8H) /
Haydn, arr. Bilbro $2.95

00406208 First Jazz (1P, 4H) /
Melody Bober.............................$2.50

Later Elementary

00415178 Changing Places (1P, 4H) /
Edna Mae Burnam $3.99

00406209 Puppy Pranks (1P, 4H) /
Melody Bober.............................$2.50

00416864 Rockin' Ragtime Boogie (1P, 4H) /
Glenda Austin.............................$3.99

00120780 Strollin' (1P, 4H) /
Carolyn Miller.............................$3.99

Early Intermediate

00113157 Dance in the City (1P, 4H) /
Naoko Ikeda $3.99

00416843 Festive Celebration (1P, 4H) /
Carolyn Miller..............................$3.99

00114960 Fountain in the Rain (1P, 4H) /
William Gillock, arr. Austin........$3.99

00416854 A Little Bit of Bach (1P, 4H) /
Glenda Austin $3.99

00158602 Reflections of You (1P, 4H) /
Randall Hartsell..........................$3.99

00416921 Tango in D Minor (IP, 4H) /
Carolyn Miller $3.99

00416955 Tango Nuevo (1P, 4H) /
Eric Baumgartner $3.99

Mid-Intermediate

00411831 Ave Maria (2P, 4H) /
Bach-Gounod, arr. Hinman........$2.95

00410726 Carmen Overture (1P, 6H) /
Bizet, arr. Sartorio.....................$3.95

00404388 Champagne Toccata (2P, 8H) /
William Gillock $3.99

00405212 Dance of the Sugar Plum Fairy /
Tchaikovsky, arr. Gillock $3.99

00416959 Samba Sensation (1P, 4H) /
Glenda Austin..............................$3.99

00405657 Valse Elegante (1P, 4H) /
Glenda Austin..............................$3.99

00149102 Weekend in Paris (1P, 4H) /
Naoko Ikeda $3.99

Later Intermediate

00415223 Concerto Americana (2P, 4H) /
John Thompson $5.99

00405552 España Cañi (1P, 4H) /
Marquina, arr. Gillock $3.99

00405409 March of the Three Kings
(1P, 4H) / *Bizet, arr. Gillock*.......$2.95

Advanced

00411832 Air (2P, 4H) / *Bach,
arr. Hinman* $2.95

00405663 Habañera (1P, 4H) /
Stephen Griebling $2.95

00405299 Jesu, Joy of Man's Desiring
(1P, 4H) / *Bach, arr. Gillock*.......$3.99

00405648 Pavane (1P, 4H) /
Fauré, arr. Carroll......................$2.95

View sample pages and
hear audio excerpts online at
www.halleonard.com.

www.willispianomusic.com

0617